Vowels

© 2015 OnBoard Academics, Inc
Portsmouth, NH
800-596-3175
www.onboardacademics.com
ISBN: 978-1-63096-027-8

OnBoard Academic's books are specifically designed to be used as printed workbooks or as on-screen instruction. Each page offers focused exercises and students quickly master topics with enough proficiency to move on to the next level.

OnBoard Academic's lessons are used in over 25,000 classrooms to rave reviews. Our lessons are aligned to the most recent governmental standards and are updated from time to time as standards change. Correlation documents are located on our website. Our lessons are created, edited and evaluated by educators to ensure top quality and real life success.

Interactive lessons for digital whiteboards, mobile devices, and PCs are available at www.onboardacademics.com. These interactive lessons make great additions to our books.

You can always reach us at customerservice@onboardacademics.com.

Short Vowel Word Families

Key Vocabulary

short a, e, i, o, and u vowel sounds

vowel

rhyme

Vowel Sounds.
Say each word slowly and circle the letter making the short vowel sound.

bat   lip   ten   cop   pup

_____

Create words with a short a vowel sounds.
If you have trouble, use the picture below each box as a hint but try to come up with your own.

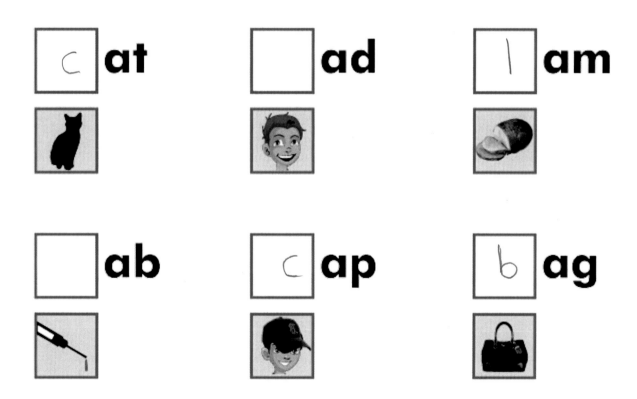

Find and circle the words with the short i vowel sound.

Pen

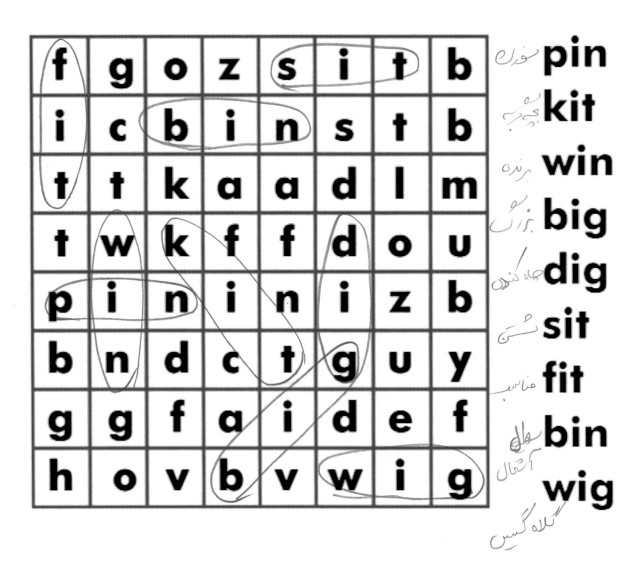

pin

kit

win

big

dig

sit

fit

bin

wig

Unscramble these short e vowel sound words.

| n | e | p | pen

| t | e | p | pet

| e | d | b | bed

| n | e | h | hen غير

Connect the rhyming words with the short o sound.
After you have connected the rhyming words write in a new rhyming word in the box provided.

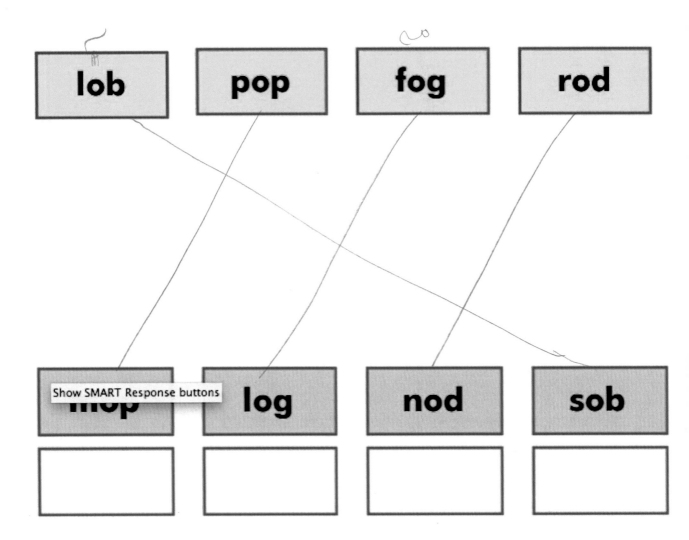

Use the clues to find the missing u short vowel sound words.

We drink milk from a [|u|] .

I gave Mom a big [|u|] .

The [|u|] crawled on my arm.

The dog was a cute [|u|] .

Pick up the toys on the [|u|] .

Sort the pictures by their short vowel sound and draw them in the correct box.

a	e	i	o	u

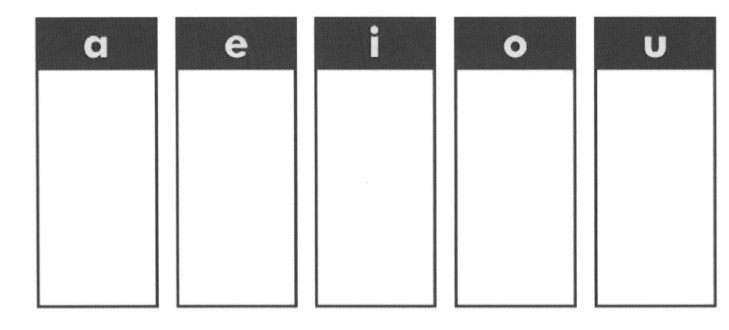

Name_____

Short Vowel Word Families Quiz

1. Ten is a short i vowel sound word. True or false?

2. Circle the word that is not a short u vowel sound word?
     a. big
     b. bug
     c. mug
     d. rug

3. Circle the missing short o vowel word from this
    sentence.
     a. log
     b. dog
     c. fog
     d. pop

4. Circle the words that rhyme with black.
     a. hat
     b. lap
     c. track
     d. trash
     e.

5. Circle the word that rhymes with jump?
     a. bump
     b. junk
     c. up
     d. luck

R-Controlled Vowel Patterns

Key Vocabulary

vowel

vowel pattern

R-Controlled Vowel Patterns

These words have r-controlled vowel patterns.

The vowel sound changes when it is followed by the letter -r.

Highlight or circle the words that have r-controlled verb patterns. Identify the verb pattern in each word and write it in the box.

The McDonald's barn sat on a hill. A lovely fern grew next to it on a rich patch of dirt. One day a storm blew in. So the little fern curled up and took a nap, dreaming of a sunny day.

_____

sir		fur	
born		herd	
hurt		third	
clerk		alarm	
guitar		torn	

11

Find a rhyme that matches each r-controlled vowel pattern.

barn	ladder	shirt	fork	burn
clatter	churn	pork	squirt	yarn

Identify words with the r-controlled verb pattern.

David's dad is the author of a book.

The story is about a bear with shiny black fur.

The first chapter is called deep in the dark woods.

Name_____

R-Controlled Vowel Pattern Quiz

1. Worm has an r-controlled vowel pattern. True or false?

2. What missing letters will complete the word: sh__k?
   a. or
   b. er
   c. ar
   d. ur

3. What missing letters will complete the word: g__l?
   a. ir
   b. er
   c. ar
   d. ur

4. Which word does not have the same r-controlled vowel
   pattern as alarm?
   a. star
   b. call
   c. scar
   d. parts

5. We ate ice cream for dess__t.
   a. ar
   b. ir
   c. er
   d. ur

Long Vowel Word Families

Key Vocabulary

vowel

long vowel sound

word families

Long Vowel Sounds

What is the sound of the first vowel in each word.

a   e   i   o   u

Vowels that say their names are called *long vowels*.

plate   **beam**   **kite**   **bone**   **cube**

☐   ☐   ☐   ☐   ☐

What makes vowel sounds long?

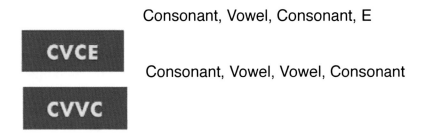

Consonant, Vowel, Consonant, E

Consonant, Vowel, Vowel, Consonant

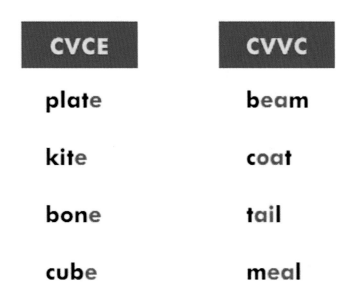

CVCE	CVVC
plate	beam
kite	coat
bone	tail
cube	meal

In a **CVCE** word, the "magic e" makes the first vowel say its name. In a **CVVC** word, the "vowel team" says the first vowel's name.

Add vowels to make CVCE words.

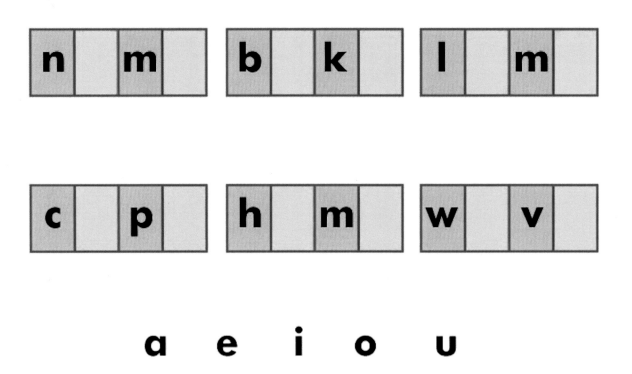

a   e   i   o   u

Use vowel teams to complete these words.

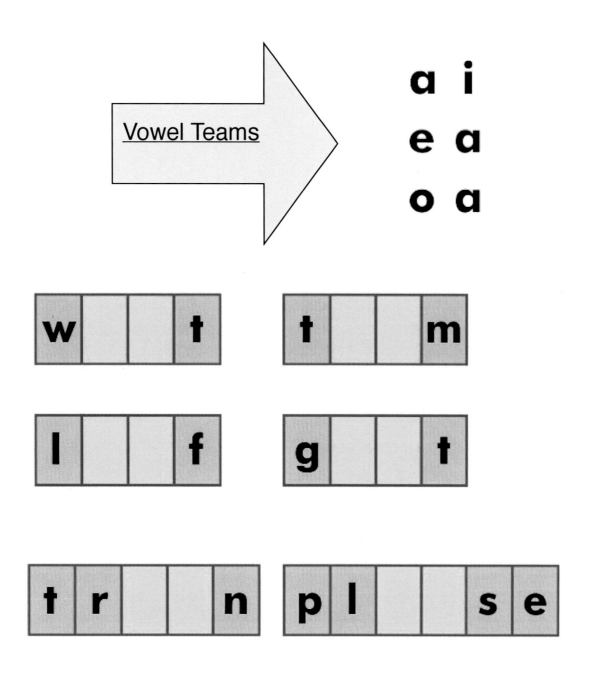

Unscramble the CVCE words.

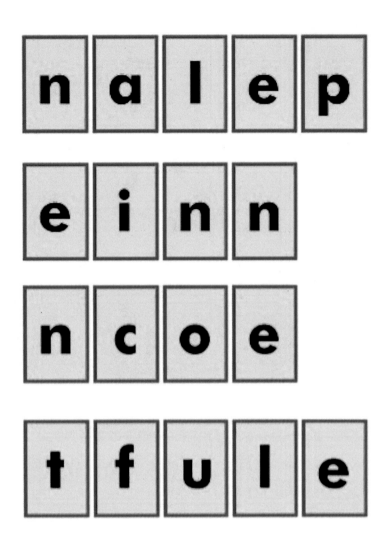

Complete the CVVC crossword puzzle.

1↓

1→

2↓   **3↓**

2→

3→

Across
1. My rubber raft helps me to _____ in the water.
2. You've got _____!
3. The boat had a bright yellow _____!

Down
1. Our _____ scored 40 points.
2. I like honey on my _____ in the morning.
3. Lambs do this - it means to jump.

Find CVCE rhyming words.

brake			ride			rope

_____

Find CVVC rhyming words.

brain			gear			boat

Name_____

Long Vowel Word Families Quiz

1. The word rain has a vowel team. True or false?

2. Circle the word with a long sound.
    a. flat
    b. car
    c. maps
    d. games

3. Circle the word with the long i sound.
    a. pin
    b. sit
    c. hike
    d. ink

4. An e at the end of a word usually makes the previous
    vowel say its name. True or false?

5. Circle the word that rhymes with brain.
    a. name
    b. same
    c. cave
    d. train

Short Vowel Sounds

Key Vocabulary

short vowel

short vowel sound

Do your recognize these sounds? Say them out loud.

 AAAAAAH! That hurts.

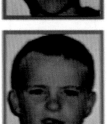 eh? What did you say?

 iiiiiiiiiih! That's yucky.

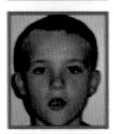 OOOOOOOOOOOO. The ferry horn sounds like this.

 uuu? I'm not sure.

Short vowel sounds.
Now lets use those sounds with words.

	ă	ăpple
	ĕ	ĕgg
	ĭ	ĭgloo
	ŏ	ŏlive
	ŭ	ŭmbrella

Say the words and listen for the short vowel sound.

Match the vowels with the pictures.

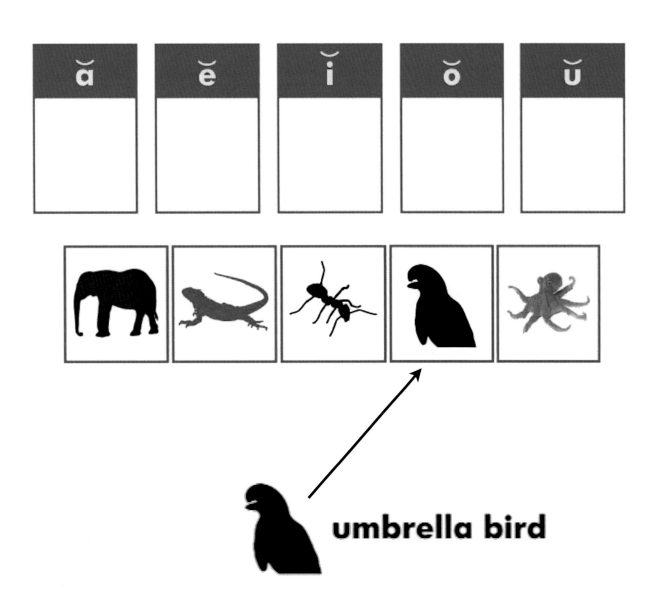

umbrella bird

Write in the missing vowel for these short vowel sound words.

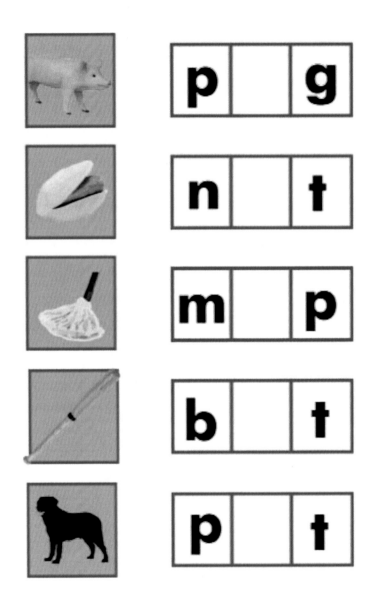

Think about other short vowel sound words and fill in the boxes.

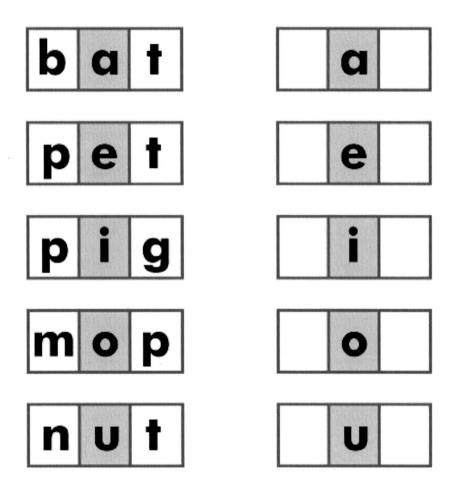

Circle the vowels with short vowel sounds.
Hint; there are 18.

Jack and Jill went up the hill
to fetch a pail of
water. Jack fell
down and broke
his crown, and Jill
came tumbling after.

a   e   i   o   u

Name_____

Short Vowel Sounds Quiz

1. Nut is a word with a short vowel sound. True or false?

2. What is the missing vowel for this short vowel sound word?

d __ g

3. Circle the words contains a short vowel sound?
   a. rat
   b. grape
   c. shade
   d. late

4. Which of these words contain the short i vowel sound?
   a. hide
   b. shine
   c. hill
   d. five

5. Which of these words contain the short e vowel sound?
   a. rest
   b. eat
   c. grccn
   d. we

Vowel Teams

Key Vocabulary

vowel

vowel teams

When two vowels go together they are a......

_____

Sort these cards by sound.
Write the vowel teams that make the same sound in a circle togther

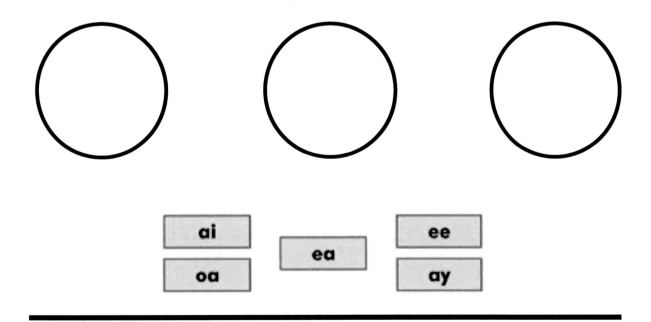

Match the vowel team with the correct illustration.

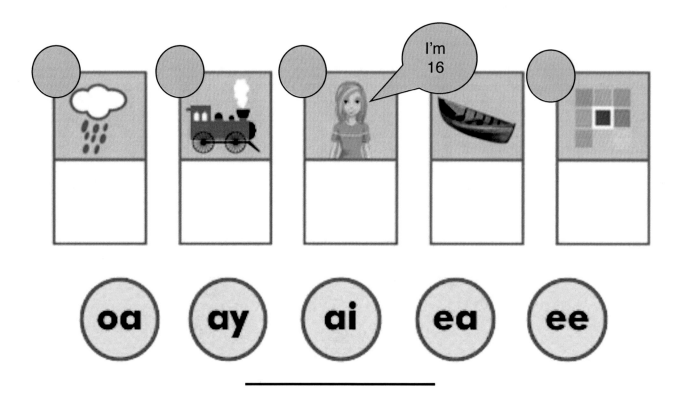

Use vowel teams to complete these words.

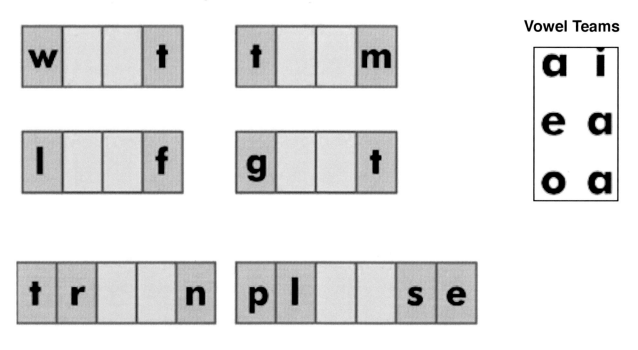

Vowel Teams

a	i
e	a
o	a

Vowel Team Word Search

t	g	h	m	i	v	e	k	d	t
r	g	h	a	e	g	d	y	d	a
a	v	n	e	a	t	i	k	d	o
i	r	a	t	k	d	b	n	k	l
l	c	e	q	u	m	i	g	o	f
c	k	f	e	p	l	a	y	u	r
o	e	s	e	l	v	y	k	d	y
r	n	e	d	h	o	p	g	u	t
e	l	k	b	k	c	i	d	o	t
s	c	g	f	t	s	o	a	k	t

neat

sleep

play

trail

float

soak

Complete the postcard to Owen's pal, Dieter.

Find and list rhyming words for these vowel teams.

Hi Dieter,

How have you b____n? Did you

get the em____l I sent you with

the photos? It was my birthd____

last w____k, so we went for a

m____l at my favorite restaurant.

I had a ch____se burger and an

ice cr____m fl____t. Sp____k to you

soon. All the best, Owen.

Dieter Werner

Strasse 58

70178 Stuttgart

Germany

ea	ai
oa	
ee	ay

boat	keep

train

Name_____

Vowel Teams Quiz

1. Vowel teams can include consonants and vowels. True or false?

2. Circle the vowel teams.
   a. ao
   b. ee
   c. by
   d. no

3. Circle the vowel teams with the same sound.
   a. ay
   b. ee
   c. oa
   d. ai

4. List 5 words with vowel teams.
   a. _____
   b. _____
   c. _____
   d. _____
   e. _____

Vowel Teams: OU, OI, and OY

Key vocabulary

Vowel team

Match the vowel team with an image by connecting them with a line.

> When two vowels are side by side, they create a new sound. This is called a vowel team. Examples of vowel teams include ou, oi, and oy.

Hints:

White puffy thing in sky   When water turns to steam   Not a girl but a _____

Sort the words by the sound of the vowel team.

Say the word in each column to hear the sound of the vowel team. Write the words into the the correct column based on the sound of their vowel team.

The vowel team ou makes two separate sounds, while the vowel teams oi and oy make the same sound.

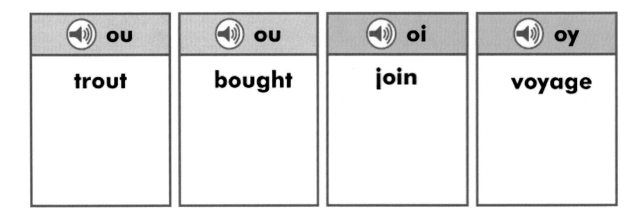

🔊 ou	🔊 ou	🔊 oi	🔊 oy
trout	bought	join	voyage

joy	convoy	account	south
voice	moisture	fought	thought

Identify the vowel team by thinking of another word with the same sound and vowel team. Write your answer in the box.

	oi	join
	oi	noise
	ou	south
	oy	oyster
	ou	camouflage
	oy	royal

ou

oy

oi

Find rhyming words for these ou, oi and oy vowel words.
Write your answer in the box provided

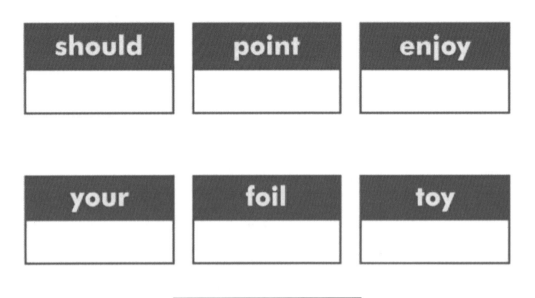

should	point	enjoy

your	foil	toy

Use vowels to complete these words

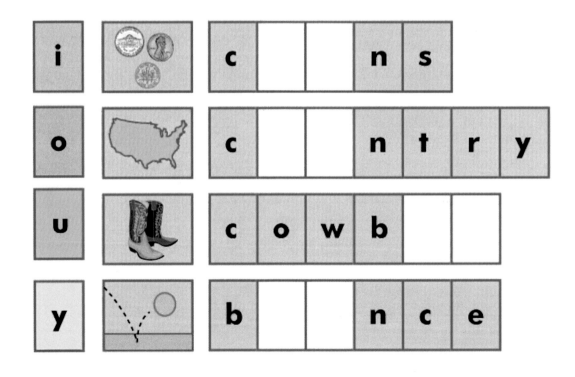

Identify the words with the vowel teams oi, oy and ou in the passage. Write your answers in the boxes provided.

The young boy was out for a walk with his hound dog. They were enjoying the sunshine as they came around the bend in the path and saw a coyote. They crouched behind a boulder hoping to avoid a confrontation.

Complete the crossword puzzle with words containing the vowel teams oi, oy and ou.

ACROSS

1. Silk is soft to the _____.

2. A type of women's shirt.

3. Where two bones connect.

4. Something to play with.

5. To cook with direct heat.

DOWN

1. Tally items.

2. There was a _____ around the construction site.

3. Another word for happiness.

4. Unpleasant sounds.

5. A pig makes this sound.

Name_____

Vowel teams: ou, oi, oy Quiz

1. True or false? OI and OY make the same sound.

2. Circle the vowel teams that make the sound in this word: COILED. OA, OI, OY, OU

3. You might live in a building made for a single family called a _____. What vowel team is in that word? _____

4. If a boat didn't _____ on the water it would sink. What vowel team is in your answer?

5. Circle your answer. He b__nced the ball. OA, OI, OY, OU

6. The girl said to the boy, "Stop making that sound. It ann___s me."

Vowel Patterns: EW, UE, AW, and AU

Key Vocabulary

Vowel Patterns

Vowel

Find the missing letters.

  Anthony bl_____ his nose in a tiss_____.

  My mom t_____ght me how to dr_____ a cat.

| a | e | u | w |

Circle the word with the vowel pattern ew, ue, aw and au and then identify the vowel pattern by writing it in the box.

The T-Rex is Mia's favorite dinosaur. □

Mildew likes to grow in damp places. □

The car continued down the road. □

That movie was awesome! □

An awful smell came from the garbage. □

That piece of jewelry is fantastic. □

| ew | ue | aw | au |

Complete the vowel patterns for these words.

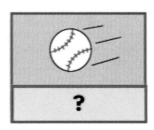

d_____t   _____tumn   thr_____   p_____

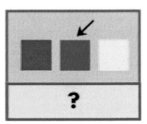

ch_____   r_____w   _____to   bl_____

www.onboardacademics.com

Say the word in each column and listen to the sound the vowel pattern makes.
Add all the other words to the column that have the same sound.

haul   **audio**   **true**

cue   **hawk**   **knew**

Rhyme the words with the same vowel pattern sound.
Write the rhyming words next to each other in the boxes provided.

		hue	cause
		saw	flaw
		clause	few
		duel	pawn
		lawn	due
		cruel	flew

Spell and say the word.   After you spell and say the word, write the vowel pattern in the boxes provided.

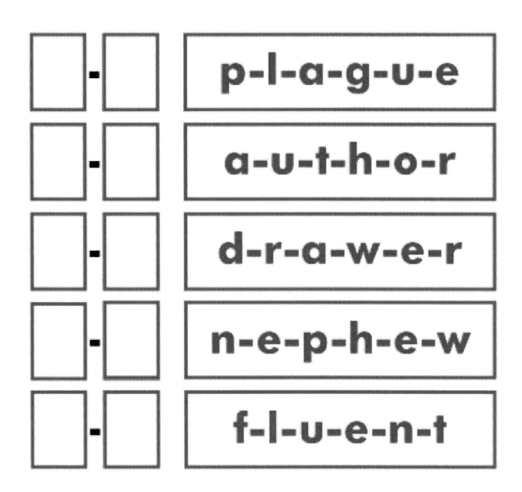

Name_____

Vowel Pattern Quiz

1. True or false? The vowel patterns ew and au make the same sound.

Say these words aloud to listen for the vowel pattern.
2.What is the vowel pattern in the word HAWK?

   _____

3.What is the vowel pattern in the word AVENUE?

   _____

4.What is the vowel pattern in the word STEW?

   _____

5.What is the vowel pattern in the word GLUE?

   _____

6.What is the vowel pattern in the word TAUGHT?

   _____

Manufactured by Amazon.ca
Acheson, AB

10990885R00033